BLACK HISTORY MAKERS

Sports People

Adam Sutherland

Black History Makers: Sports People is an introduction to some of black history's most prolific sports people, all of whom have successfully changed the face of their sport. Sport is a universal activity and through the determination, dedication and respect for key sports people, the world unites to join together nations, faiths and races.

The sports men and women in this book have broken down racial barriers, not only for themselves but for future generations, and always with the hope and dream of passing on the baton to the sports people of the future, so that they can go forth and achieve new and even greater heights.

Never before has the world been so proud to observe and wonder at our black sports heroes and heroines, who are breaking down barriers and breaking world records, setting the world alight with their achievements. We salute you and cheer you on!

Mia Morris OBE, Black History Mon...

Published in 2013 by Wayland
Copyright © Wayland 2013

Wayland
338 Euston Road
London NW1 3BH

Wayland Australia
Level 17/207 Kent Street
Sydney, NSW 2000

All rights reserved.

Editor: Katie Woolley
Designer: Tim Mayer, MayerMedia
Consultant: Mia Morris, Black History Month website

British Library Cataloguing in Publication Data

Sutherland, Adam.
  Sports people. -- (Black history makers)
  1. Athletes, Black--Biography--Juvenile literature.
  I. Title II. Series
  796'.0922-dc22

ISBN: 978 0 7502 7874 4

Printed in China

10 9 8 7 6 5 4 3 2 1

Wayland is a division of Hachette Children's Books,
an Hachette UK company. www.hachette.co.uk

Picture acknowledgements
Derek Cattani/Rex Features: 5, Eyre Crowe/Bridgeman Art Library/
Getty Images: 4, John Dominis/Time-Life Pictures/Getty Images: 8,
Fox Photos/Getty Images: 6, Lynn Goldsmith/Corbis: 10,
Louise Gubb/CORBIS SABA/Corbis: 9, Hulton Archive/Getty Images: 11,
Keystone/Getty Images: 7, David Madison/New Sport/Corbis: 23BL,
Clive Mason/ALLSPORT/Getty Images: 23BR, Daniel Munoz/Reuters/
Corbis: COVER, 17, PA/PA Archive/Press Association Images: 23TR,
Steven R. Schaefer/AFP/Getty Images: 23BC, Michael Steele/Getty
Images: 13, Bob Thomas/Getty Images: 3, 21, Courtesy Geoff
Thompson: 23TC, Jerry Wachter/Sports Imagery/Getty Images: 12,
Ian Walton/Getty Images: 23TL, Shutterstock: Title page, 14, 15, 16, 18,
19, 20

CONTENTS

Words in **bold** can be found in the glossary on page 24.

Making History

For nearly 200 years, from the early 1600s to the 1800s, slaves were brought from Africa and sold in slave markets. This slave trade brought more than four million African slaves to the United States of America (USA) to work on large coffee and sugar **plantations** in the American south. The US Civil War (1861–65) was fought partly to end slavery in the USA, but even when it was **abolished** in 1865, **segregation** and **racial prejudice** remained for many years.

Fighting prejudice

Black athletes have had to face the same struggles that all of black history has faced and achieving success hasn't always been easy. The athletes featured in this book have had to fight **economic** and social segregation and racial prejudice – as well as their opponents – to reach the top of their chosen sporting profession.

These slaves are waiting to be sold at a slave market.

Olympic success and failure

These struggles continued for many years and even by the 1930s, successful black athletes were rare and a black Olympic champion like Jesse Owens (page 6) was one in a million. Jesse's four gold medals at the 1936 Berlin Olympic Games were all the more important because he was competing against Adolf Hitler's plans to produce a white German 'super race'. Jesse may have struck a blow against **racism** in Germany, but he continued to face racial problems back in the USA.

Black power

The late 1960s and early 1970s was the era of '**black power**' in the USA – this was the embracing of black pride and identity and the advancement of black values by a generation of African Americans.

Although not formally associated with the movement, heavyweight boxer Muhammad Ali (page 10) showed the world what it meant to be black and proud. Ali's intelligence and showmanship, as well as his abilities in the ring and his refusal to fight for a 'white' US Army against the 'black' Vietnamese, made him a perfect role model for the cause.

Continued racial discrimination

Some sports became racially **desegregated** more quickly than others. The first African American to sign a National Basketball Association (NBA) contract was Nat Clifton in 1950. In golf, by contrast, the Augusta National Golf Club in Georgia – a club that hosts one of the sport's four 'Major' tournaments every year – did not accept black members until 1990.

Looking to the future

It is now nearly 100 years since our first black sporting history maker, Jesse Owens, was born. A lot of changes have taken place since then and black sports men and women around the world can finally stand shoulder to shoulder with their white competitors.

Sprinters Tommie Smith (centre) and John Carlos (right) gave the 'Black Power' movement's famous 'Black Power Salute' at the 1968 Olympic Games.

Jesse Owens
The World Beater

James Cleveland Owens was the seventh of eleven children. At nine, a schoolteacher misheard his name 'JC' as 'Jesse' and the nickname stuck. Young Jesse developed his passion for running thanks to the support and encouragement of his school coach, Charles Riley. Jesse's family were poor, so he delivered groceries and worked in a shoe repair shop to help put food on the table.

Name: James Cleveland 'Jesse' Owens

Born: September 12, 1913, Oakville, Alabama, USA

Died: March 31, 1980

Sport: Athletics

Awards and titles: Four gold medals at the 1936 Olympic Games, set world records in the long jump, 220-yard sprint and 220-yard hurdles.

Interesting fact: Has an asteroid named after him – 6758 Jesseowens.

Jesse enjoyed success in the 1936 Olympic Games in Berlin, Germany, but was unable to compete as an **amateur** athelete again.

Highs and lows

In 1933, while at high school in Cleveland, Jesse equalled the world record of 9.4 seconds in the 100-yard dash. Jesse became a hot property, and Ohio State University helped his father find a job so Jesse could study and train there. In 1935, Jesse set three world records and equalled a fourth all in one day. These successes did not change his social status, however. Because of racial segregation – the legal separation of American blacks and whites – Jesse had to live off-campus with other black athletes. When he travelled with the team he ate in 'black-only' restaurants and slept in 'black-only' hotels.

> " I wasn't invited to shake hands with Hitler, [but] I wasn't invited to the White House to shake hands with the President either. "
>
> *Jesse Owens*

Jesse Owens's four gold medals at the 1936 Olympics put him in the history books

World beater

The Berlin Olympics in 1936 made Jesse a legend. He won gold medals in the 100-metre sprint, long jump, 200-metre sprint and 4 x 100 metres relay. However, as an amateur sportsman, Jesse received no prize money for his wins. So, when he was offered 'appearance money' to compete in specially organised events, Jesse couldn't turn it down. A poor man all his life, the temptation to earn some money for his family was too great.

Until recently, sporting competitions like the Olympics were only open to amateur athletes who did not get paid to compete. Being paid to race therefore, made Jesse a professional and US athletic officials withdrew his amateur status.

Unable to compete again against the world's best, Jesse travelled widely, making speeches to many youth groups and corporate organisations and continued to inspire people until his death in 1980.

MAKING HISTORY

Just before the 1936 Games, Jesse was visited at the Olympic Village by Adi Dassler, the founder of Adidas, who persuaded Jesse to run in Adidas shoes. It was the first sponsorship of a male African American athlete in history.

Kipchoge Keino
The Inspirational Runner

Name: Kipchoge 'Kip' Keino

Born: January 17, 1940, Kipsamo, Nandi District, Kenya

Sport: Athletics

Awards and titles: Gold medals at the 1968 and 1972 Olympics and Chairman of the Kenyan Olympic Committee since 1999.

Interesting fact: In the Nandi language Kipchoge means 'born near the grain storage shed'.

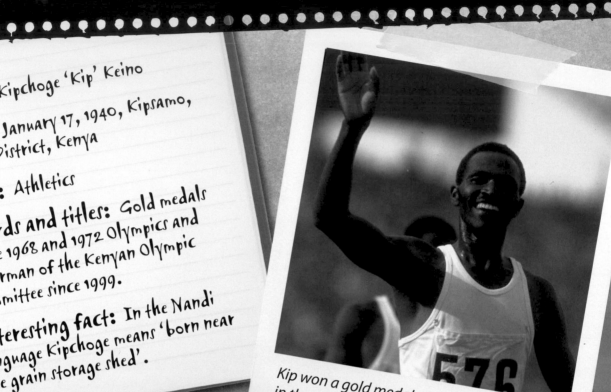

Kip won a gold medal at the 1972 Olympics in the 10,000 metre race.

Early life

Kip Keino was born into a group of the Kalenjin tribe called the Nandi, in Kenya. As a youngster, Kip herded goats on Kenya's hilly countryside and used his spare time to practise running. His father, a long-distance runner himself, encouraged his son in the sport. This **high-altitude** training, where the oxygen content in the air is lower, provided Kip with great **stamina**.

Fighting spirit

After both his parents died, Kip was brought up by an aunt and when he left school, Kip joined the Kenyan police. He continued to run in his spare time however, and in 1964, he broke onto the world stage, setting two world records in the 3,000 metres and 5,000 metres races.

By 1965, he was travelling around the world to race and at the 1966 Commonwealth Games he won gold in the mile and three-mile races.

Olympic glory

Kip arrived at the 1968 Olympics in Mexico City with stomach pains that were later diagnosed as a severe bladder infection. However, he still managed to lead the 10,000 metres until he collapsed with two laps to go. He was helped to his feet and finished the race, but was later disqualified for leaving the track.

Kip has devoted his life to helping those less fortunate than himself in his home country. Here, he is jogging across the Kenyan countryside with orphans in 1996.

On the day of the 1,500 metres final, doctors told Kip he was still too ill to race, but he decided that he owed it to his country to at least compete. Kip was caught in traffic on the way to the stadium. He got out of the car and ran the last mile to the stadium, before completing the race in first place in an Olympic record time!

Helping children

After retiring from the sport in 1975, Kip and his wife Phyllis set up an orphanage, the Kip Keino Children's Home. The project has now grown to include the Kip Keino School, teaching almost 300 children aged 6–13. Kip is also Chairman of the Kenyan Olympic Committee. In 1996, he joined the World Sports **Humanitarian** Hall of Fame.

MAKING HISTORY

Kip Keino's Olympic success inspired the country's dominance of long distance running. Since 1968, Kenya has won every 3,000-metre Olympic steeplechase it has entered. Kenya ranks near the bottom worldwide in every social and economic category – life expectancy, **per capita income**, child mortality – but on the track, thanks to Kip, it has become number one.

Muhammad Ali

The Greatest

Born Cassius Clay in rural Kentucky, the young Cassius started boxing under local trainer Fred Stoner. Fast and strong, he excelled at the sport and blazed a trail through the amateur ranks, winning six Kentucky titles, two national titles, and a Light Heavyweight gold medal at the 1960 Olympics in Rome, Italy. After his Olympic triumph, he turned professional and progressed steadily through the ranks, winning his first 19 professional fights. This success earned him the right to fight World Champion Sonny Liston in February 1964.

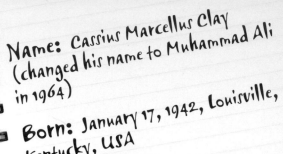

Name: Cassius Marcellus Clay (changed his name to Muhammad Ali in 1964)

Born: January 17, 1942, Louisville, Kentucky, USA

Sport: Boxing

Awards and titles: Olympic gold medal, three World Heavyweight titles and voted BBC Sports Personality of the Century.

Interesting fact: One of Ali's fights inspired Sylvester Stallone to write the original Rocky film.

Muhammad Ali was a world star both in and out of the boxing ring.

Religious beliefs

After defeating Liston, Cassius announced that he had become a Muslim and had been given the name Muhammad Ali. He continued boxing and successfully defended his title several times. However, in 1967, he was called up to fight for the US Army in the Vietnam War but refused to serve. Ali was stripped of his heavyweight title and his boxing licence and did not fight again for three years. He made a living speaking at anti-war gatherings at colleges and universities around the country.

> 66 Hating people because of their colour is wrong... It doesn't matter which colour does the hating. It's just plain wrong. 99
>
> *Muhammad Ali*

Muhammad Ali (then Cassius Clay) won his first world title in 1964, beating Sonny Liston.

Big fights

In 1970, Ali was granted a new licence and stepped back into the ring. The final stage of his career was by far the most memorable. He fought – and defeated – fellow heavyweight champions Joe Frazier and George Foreman in some of the best-remembered boxing matches of all time. In a professional career from 1960–1981, Ali won 56 fights and lost only five. After retiring from the sport, he was diagnosed with **Parkinson's disease**. Despite the illness, Ali remains an active public figure today. He has been on Middle Eastern peace missions with the United Nations and been presented with peace medals for his humanitarian efforts.

MAKING HISTORY

Muhammad Ali was the best known black sportsman of his day. His intelligence and achievements gave young black people a role model to identify with. As a prominent black Muslim, he also helped to raise understanding of his religion and beliefs.

Michael Jordan
Basketball Superhero

Michael Jordan grew up in Wilmington, North Carolina, USA and attended the University of North Carolina, where he excelled at basketball. He was named Player of the Year and scored the winning basket in the 1982 college championships.

Name: Michael Jeffrey Jordan

Born: February 17, 1963, Brooklyn, New York, USA

Sport: Basketball

Awards and titles: Six NBA Championships with the Chicago Bulls and voted greatest North American athlete of the 20th century by ESPN.

Interesting fact: Michael had a trainer made in his honour, the Nike Air Jordan.

Jordan competing against Washington for the Chicago Bulls in 1991.

> 66 I realise that I'm black, but I like to be viewed as a person and this is everybody's wish. 99

Michael Jordan

Success in the NBA

He joined the Chicago Bulls in 1982 and quickly emerged as the best player the league had ever seen. His jumping abilities earned him the nickname 'Air Jordan'. With Michael in the team, the Bulls won six NBA titles and Michael himself was named the league's Most Valuable Player five times.

Making history

In 2000, Michael Jordan was named ESPN Athlete of the Century. His popularity brought new fans and advertisers to the sport and the current generation of NBA stars credit him as their inspiration for taking up the sport.

Kelly Holmes
The Golden Girl

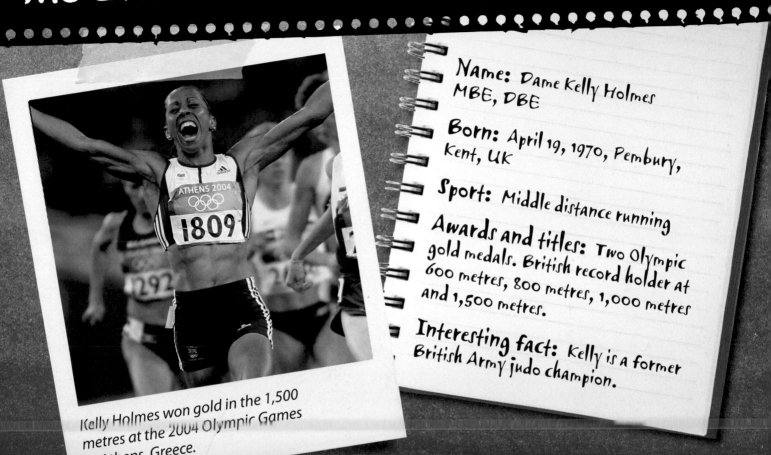

Kelly Holmes won gold in the 1,500 metres at the 2004 Olympic Games in Athens, Greece.

Name: Dame Kelly Holmes MBE, DBE

Born: April 19, 1970, Pembury, Kent, UK

Sport: Middle distance running

Awards and titles: Two Olympic gold medals. British record holder at 600 metres, 800 metres, 1,000 metres and 1,500 metres.

Interesting fact: Kelly is a former British Army judo champion.

Kelly Holmes started running at 12 years old and won the English Schools 1,500 metres title the following year. However, she turned her back on athletics at 18 to join the Army. At first she drove trucks before retraining as a PE training instructor and rose to the rank of sergeant.

Back to athletics

Kelly returned to the track in 1992, becoming national champion in the 800 metres in 1993. Injuries and ill-health kept her out of the medals until the Athens Olympics in 2004. Kelly won victories in the 800 metres and 1,500 metres.

She retired in 2005 and is currently fronting the government's School Olympics initiative to get competitive sport back into the playground.

MAKING HISTORY

In 2009, Kelly Holmes established the DKH Legacy Trust, which encourages young people to take part and excel in sport and helps disadvantaged young people to find and believe in their own talents. Kelly also played an important role in London's winning bid to host the 2012 Olympic Games.

Tiger Woods
Golfing Phenomenon

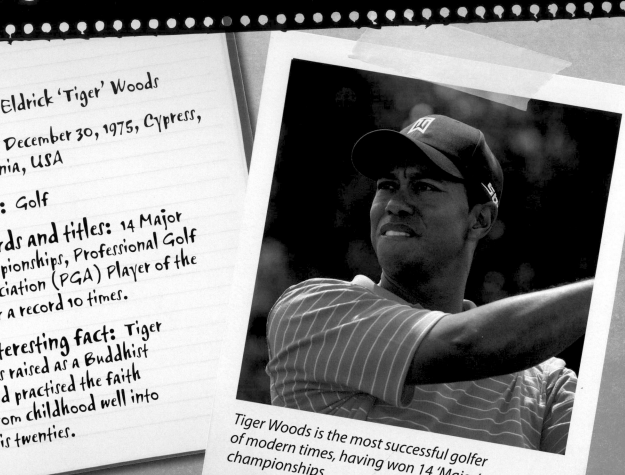

Name: Eldrick 'Tiger' Woods

Born: December 30, 1975, Cypress, California, USA

Sport: Golf

Awards and titles: 14 Major championships, Professional Golf Association (PGA) Player of the Year a record 10 times.

Interesting fact: Tiger was raised as a Buddhist and practised the faith from childhood well into his twenties.

Tiger Woods is the most successful golfer of modern times, having won 14 'Major' championships.

Childhood talent

Tiger Woods was introduced to golf at two years old by his father, Earl. The same year he entered, and won, a local tournament for Under 10s! By the age of three he was playing on adult golf courses, at five he was appearing on national US television and at eight he won the first of six Junior World Golf Championships. He was also the first golfer to win the US Amateur title three years in a row.

Major achievements

Tiger earned a golf scholarship to the prestigious Stanford University but left after just two years to turn professional. Professional golf is historically a white sport. One of the most famous courses, Augusta National in Georgia, only accepted its first African American member in 1990. Fortunately, Tiger Woods's talent helped to turn this prejudice on its head.

> **"** Growing up, I came up with this name: I'm a 'Cablinasian'. As in Caucasian-black-Indian-Asian. I'm just who I am. **"**
>
> *Tiger Woods*

Majors

There are four 'Major' golf tournaments every year that all golfers want to win more than any others – the US Masters, US PGA, British Open and US Open. Nine months after turning professional, Tiger won his first Major at the US Masters with a record score, becoming the youngest ever winner and the first African American to win.

Hot property

Tiger Woods has single-handedly expanded golf's popularity. His amazing golfing success and broad public appeal have made him one of the world's most recognisable athletes. Tiger continues to compete and hopes to one day match veteran player Jack Nicklaus's 18 Major victories.

Tiger Woods playing in Bangkok, Thailand in November 2010.

Venus and Serena Williams

Record-breaking Sisters

Venus and Serena Williams starting playing tennis at four years old. It was their father Richard's dream that one day both girls would become professional tennis players. At the time, the family lived in the violent Compton district of Los Angeles, USA and the sisters practised on damaged public courts.

Names: Venus Ebony Starr Williams, Serena Jameka Williams

Born: Venus: June 17, 1980, Lynwood, California, USA

Serena: September 26, 1981, Saginaw, Michigan, USA

Sport: Tennis

Awards and titles: Venus: 9 Grand Slam singles titles, 11 doubles titles. Serena: 13 Grand Slam singles titles, 11 doubles titles.

Interesting fact: Venus has a faster average serve than Roger Federer and Rafael Nadal.

Venus (left) and Serena are known for their colourful tennis outfits and eye-catching hairstyles on the court.

> ❝ You have to believe in yourself when no one else does. That makes you a winner right there. ❞

Tennis childhood

Richard and his then-wife Oracene (now Oracene Price) were so keen for Venus and Serena to pursue tennis careers that they moved the family to Florida to enrol the girls at a tennis academy. However, their parents didn't agree with the academy's intensive methods and decided to coach the girls themselves. Richard even gave up his job in a security firm to coach them full-time. Eventually Richard's dream came true: at 17, Venus reached the final of the US Open at her first attempt and two years later, Serena, also 17, won it.

Super skills

Both sisters are tall and very strong, with powerful serves (Venus has the fastest serve in women's tennis, Serena has the second fastest), great forehands and backhands, good volleys and accurate baseline games. Between them, Venus and Serena are first and second all-time money winners in female sport with around $30m (£20m) each.

Serena (left) and Venus are a formidable team in any doubles championship. Here they are competing and winning a match in the 2009 Australian Open Doubles Championship.

Helping hands

Both are also committed workers for charity. Serena helped fund the Serena Williams Secondary School in Kenya and has supported programmes focusing on 'at risk' young people. Venus works alongside her mother helping The Owl Foundation, which supports children with learning disabilities.

MAKING HISTORY

In tennis, the world's best players measure themselves against success in four 'Grand Slams' — the Australian Open, French Open, Wimbledon and the US Open. Between them, Venus and Serena Williams have won a massive 22 Grand Slam singles titles and competed together to win a further 11 doubles titles.

> **If you can keep playing tennis when somebody is shooting a gun down the street, that's concentration.**
>
> *Serena*

Lewis Hamilton

Racing Car Star

If one man was born for speed, it's Lewis Hamilton. Named after gold Medal winning US sprinter Carl Lewis, he started racing radio-controlled cars at six years old and a year later finished second in the national championships – for adults! Lewis's father, Anthony always supported his son. He took **redundancy** from his job as an IT manager and sometimes worked three part-time jobs to have the flexibility to attend all of Lewis's races.

Name: Lewis Carl Davidson Hamilton, MBE

Born: January 7, 1985, Stevenage, Hertfordshire, UK

Sport: Formula One racing

Awards and titles: Formula One World Champion 2008 and given an MBE in 2009.

Interesting fact: He is already the youngest championship leader, the youngest Briton to win a Grand Prix and the only driver since the series started in 1950 to finish all of his first seven races on the podium.

Lewis Hamilton burst onto the Formula One scene with a record-breaking four race wins in his debut season.

Young dreams

At ten years old, Lewis met McLaren boss Ron Dennis and told him, "One day I want to be racing your cars...". Dennis wrote in Lewis's autograph book, "Call me in nine years, we'll sort something out." In 1998, Dennis made good on his promise five years early, signing Lewis to the McLaren driver development program.

World champion

With his combination of lightning-fast reflexes and a burning desire to succeed, Lewis excelled at all levels of motor racing. He has been a winner at every stage of his driving career – through British Formula Renault (where he was UK series champion in 2003) and Formula Three Euroseries (where he was Drivers' Champion in 2005) to Formula One, where he finished second in his first season (2007) and became the sport's youngest World Champion in 2008. One hundred per cent professional, hard-working and dedicated to his sport, Lewis is destined for many more years of success.

Lewis takes a corner at great speed during the 2009 Malaysian Grand Prix.

> 66 Being black is not a negative. It's a positive... because I'm different... It can open doors to different cultures and that is what motor sport is trying to do. 99

Lewis Hamilton

MAKING HISTORY

Black role models in motor racing were non-existent until Lewis Hamilton, son of a white mother and black father, set his sights on Formula One success. The first black driver in Formula One, Lewis has opened up an historically 'white' sport to a wider audience, inspiring youngsters everywhere to follow in his footsteps.

Usain Bolt

Lightning Bolt

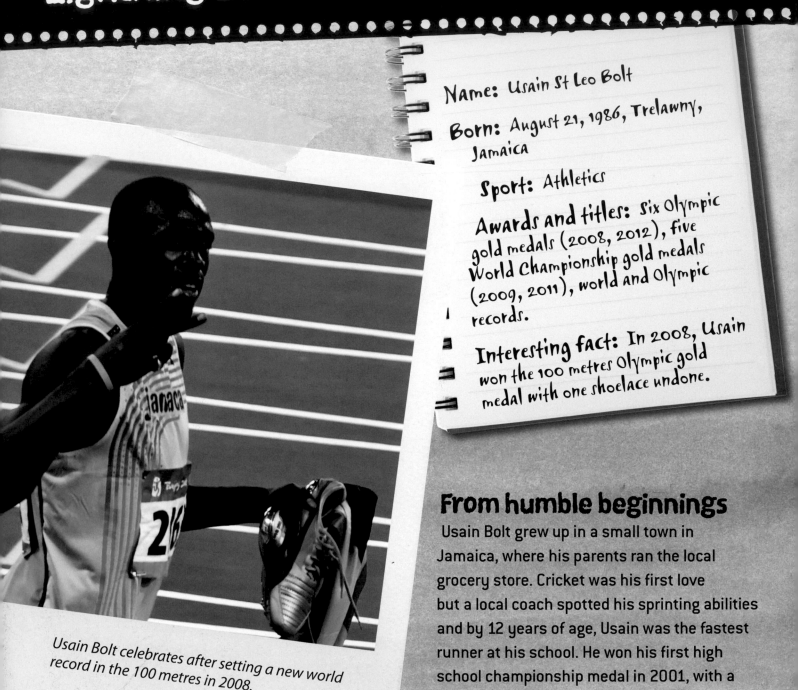

Name: Usain St Leo Bolt

Born: August 21, 1986, Trelawny, Jamaica

Sport: Athletics

Awards and titles: Six Olympic gold medals (2008, 2012), five World Championship gold medals (2009, 2011), world and Olympic records.

Interesting fact: In 2008, Usain won the 100 metres Olympic gold medal with one shoelace undone.

Usain Bolt celebrates after setting a new world record in the 100 metres in 2008.

From humble beginnings

Usain Bolt grew up in a small town in Jamaica, where his parents ran the local grocery store. Cricket was his first love but a local coach spotted his sprinting abilities and by 12 years of age, Usain was the fastest runner at his school. He won his first high school championship medal in 2001, with a silver in the 200 metres and a time of 22.04 seconds. He then competed in the 2002 Junior World Championships in Kingston, Jamaica. He won the 200 metres in a personal best time and became the youngest ever world junior gold medallist.

Olympic success

Injury affected Usain's performances at the 2004 Olympics but at Beijing in 2008 he set the world alight. He won the 100 metres in a world record 9.69 seconds, an achievement that was made even more remarkable because he visibly slowed before the line to celebrate his victory!

He then set new world and Olympic records of 19.30 seconds in the 200 metres and was part of the gold medal-winning 4 x 100 metres relay team. All three titles were defended at the London 2012 Olympics, with new world and Olympics records for the relay team. Usain was the first man to win double sprint gold since Carl Lewis in 1984.

World Beater! Usain Bolt wins gold in the 100 metres at the 2008 Olympics in Beijing, China.

World Championships

In 2009 in Berlin, Usain repeated his success with gold medals in the 100 metres, 200 metres and 4 x 100 metres relay. In the 100 metres and 200 metres, he beat his own world records with times of 9.58 seconds and 19.19 seconds. Bolt's 7-foot stride means he runs the 100 metres in just 41 steps, five less than his nearest opponent. Usain Bolt is the undisputed fastest man on earth.

MAKING HISTORY

With a population of just 2.6 million, Jamaica has an amazing tradition of Olympic sprinting success since entering their first Games in 1948. Usain Bolt is following in the footsteps of medal winners Arthur Wint, Don Quarrie and Merlene Ottey. His record-breaking runs are inspiring young Jamaicans to take to athletics, rather than basketball, football or other sports that compete for their attention. Bolt's success ensures that a new crop of Jamaican athletes will compete on the world stage for years to come.

More Sporting Heroes

The Honourable Sir Garfield St Aubrun 'Gary' Sobers (1936–)

This former West Indies cricket captain is known as the sport's greatest-ever all-rounder. Born in Bridgetown, Barbados, he played for the West Indies for 20 years, from 1954–1974, setting numerous records for his achievements. He was knighted in 1975 for his services to cricket.

Edison Arantes do Nascimento 'Pele' (1940–)

Pele was born in Tres Coracoes, Brazil and is the all-time leading goal scorer of the Brazilian national team. Fast, powerful and able to shoot with both feet, he scored 1,283 goals in a career that lasted from 1956–1977. He is the only player to be part of three World Cup-winning teams (1958, 1962, 1970).

Theresa Ione 'Tessa' Sanderson CBE (1956–)

This gold medal-winning javelin thrower was born in Jamaica but emigrated to England and competed for the UK. She appeared in a record six Olympic Games and was the first black woman to win an Olympic gold medal in 1984.

Mr Geoff Thompson MBE (1958–)

Geoff was five times WUKO World Karate Champion from 1982–1986 and the highest competitive point scorer in the history of the sport. For the past 15 years, Geoff has led the Youth Charter, a charity fighting gang culture and anti-social youth behaviour around the world.

Dikembe Mutombo (1966–)

Dikembe is a retired Congolese-American basketball player. Dikembe played for teams including the New York Knicks (2003–04) and the Houston Rockets (2004–09). He has donated millions of dollars to improve living conditions in Congo and is a Youth Emissary for the United Nations.

Marlon Shirley (1978–)

This athlete is the first T44 class athlete (missing one leg below the knee) to break 11 seconds for the 100 metres. Marlon was abandoned by his mother and lived in orphanages. He lost his leg at the age of five in an accident but athletics got Marlon's life back on track. He won gold in the 100 metres in the 2000 and 2004 Paralympics.

Timeline

1936 Jesse Owens wins four Olympic gold medals in Berlin

1958 Gary Sobers scores a record 365 not out against Pakistan

1964 Cassius Clay beats Sonny Liston to become World Heavyweight Champion

1968 Kip Keino wins an Olympic gold medal in the 1500 metres in Mexico City

1968 Olympic medal winners Tommie Smith and John Carlos give a 'Black Power Salute' on the podium in Mexico City

1970 Pele captains Brazil to World Cup victory against Italy

1974 Muhammad Ali beats George Foreman to regain his World Heavyweight title

1982 Geoff Thompson wins the first of five consecutive WUKO World Karate Championships

1984 Tessa Sanderson is the first black woman to win an Olympic gold medal

1991 Michael Jordan wins the first of six NBA Championships

1995 Dikembe Mutombo wins NBA Defensive Player of the Year award

1997 Tiger Woods wins his first 'Major' at the US Masters

1999 Serena Williams wins the US Open

2000 Venus Williams wins Wimbledon

2000 Marlon Shirley wins gold in 100 metres in the T44 (single amputee) category at the Sydney Paralympics

2004 Kelly Holmes wins gold medals in 800 metres and 1500 metres at the Athens Olympics

2004 Marlon Shirley wins gold in 100 metres, silver in the 200 metres and bronze in the long jump T44 category at the Athens Paralympics

2008 Usain Bolt wins three gold medals at the Beijing Olympics

2008 Lewis Hamilton becomes Formula One World Champion

2009 Usain Bolt wins three gold medals at the World Championships

2012 Usain Bolt and the Williams sisters all win gold medals at the London Olympics.

Legacy

The legacies of the sports people in this book live on, not only in their achievements but also through the charities they and their families have founded:

The Tiger Woods Foundation: http://web.tigerwoodsfoundation.org/index
Established by Tiger and his father Earl. The charity focuses on projects for children, from golf clinics to university scholarships.

The Muhammad Ali Centre: http://www.alicenter.org/Pages/default.aspx
Its message, according to Ali, is 'peace, social responsibility, respect and personal growth'.

The Serena Williams Foundation: http://theswf.org/
Set up to provide education and support for children from underprivileged backgrounds, and those affected by violent crime.

The DKH Legacy Trust: http://www.dkhlegacytrust.org/
The charity's team of Olympians, Paralympians, World, Commonwealth and European Champions, work with children to 'create chances for young people'.

Glossary

Index

Abolish To put an end to something, for example abolish slavery.

Amateur A sportsman or woman who does not get paid to compete in their chosen sport.

Black power A movement in 1960s America that united black people by emphasising pride in their race's achievements.

Desegregated An end to racial separation.

Economic A term relating to the finances of a country or an individual.

High-altitude An area that is high above sea level.

Humanitarian A person who wants to help to improve the welfare and happiness of others.

Parkinson's disease A disease believed to be caused by the deterioration of a person's brain cells. Sufferers often experience trembling of the fingers and hands and slow speech.

Per capita income The average amount of money earned by each person in the country.

Plantation A large estate or farm where crops are grown and tended to by workers.

Racial prejudice The belief that people from different races do not deserve the same rights, freedoms or respect as your own race.

Racism Hatred or intolerance of another race or races.

Redundancy To give up your job and stop working.

Segregation The separation of people of different races by a country's government.

Stamina A person's strength or ability to resist tiredness.